HAPPY
...PLUS 11 MORE TOP HITS

Published by
Wise Publications
14-15 Berners Street, London W1T 3LJ, UK.

Exclusive Distributors:

Music Sales Limited
Distribution Centre, Newmarket Road,
Bury St Edmunds, Suffolk IP33 3YB, UK.

Music Sales Pty Limited
Units 3-4, 17 Willfox Street, Condell Park,
NSW 2200, Australia.

Order No. AM1008964
ISBN: 978-1-78305-563-0
This book © Copyright 2014 Wise Publications,
a division of Music Sales Limited.

Unauthorised reproduction of any part of this
publication by any means including photocopying
is an infringement of copyright.

Edited by Jenni Norey.
Cover design by Tim Field.

Printed in the EU.

PIANO • VOCAL • GUITAR

CHART HITS NOW!
HAPPY
...PLUS 11 MORE TOP HITS

WISE PUBLICATIONS
part of The Music Sales Group
London / New York / Paris / Sydney / Copenhagen / Berlin / Madrid / Hong Kong / Tokyo

Your Guarantee of Quality:

As publishers, we strive to produce every book
to the highest commercial standards.

This book has been carefully designed to minimise awkward page turns
and to make playing from it a real pleasure.

Particular care has been given to specifying acid-free, neutral-sized paper
made from pulps which have not been elemental chlorine bleached.
This pulp is from farmed sustainable forests and was produced
with special regard for the environment.

Throughout, the printing and binding have been planned to ensure a sturdy,
attractive publication which should give years of enjoyment.

If your copy fails to meet our high standards, please inform us
and we will gladly replace it.

www.musicsales.com

HAND ON HEART • OLLY MURS • 12
HAPPY • PHARRELL WILLIAMS • 19
HOW LONG WILL I LOVE YOU • ELLIE GOULDING • 28
LET ME GO • GARY BARLOW • 31
LIGHT ME UP • BIRDY • 6
LITTLE ME • LITTLE MIX • 44
LOSING SLEEP • JOHN NEWMAN • 38
SOMEWHERE ONLY WE KNOW • LILY ALLEN • 56
STORY OF MY LIFE • ONE DIRECTION • 49
TIMBER • PITBULL FEAT. KESHA • 62
TRUMPETS • JASON DERULO • 68
UNCONDITIONALLY • KATY PERRY • 73

Light Me Up

Words & Music by Thomas Hull & Jasmine Van den Bogaerde

Hand On Heart

Words & Music by Wayne Hector, Thomas Barnes, Peter Kelleher, Benjamin Kohn, Iain James & Oliver Murs

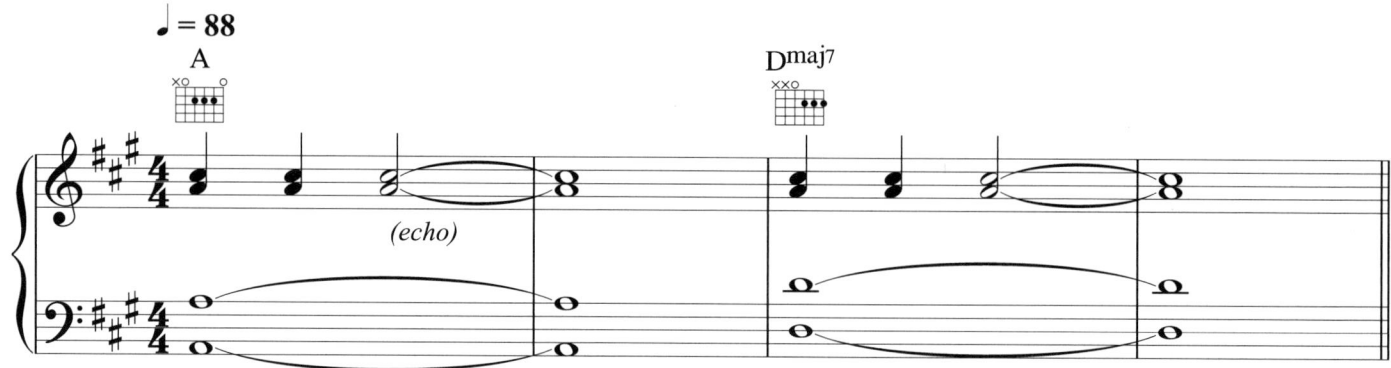

1. Come on, come on, I'm right, I'm wrong. And when I'm wrong I say,

We always had the good, the bad and that will never change.

© Copyright 2013 Salli Isaak Music Publishing Limited.
Universal Music Publishing Limited/Sony/ATV Music Publishing/Warner/Chappell Music Publishing Limited.
All Rights Reserved. International Copyright Secured.

How Long Will I Love You

Words & Music by Mike Scott

Let Me Go

Words & Music by Gary Barlow

© Copyright 2013 Sony/ATV Music Publishing.
All Rights Reserved. International Copyright Secured.

Little Me

Words & Music by Thomas Barnes, Peter Kelleher, Benjamin Kohn, Iain James,
Jessica Nelson, Jade Thirlwall, Perrie Edwards & Leigh-Anne Pinnock

© Copyright 2013 Universal Music Publishing Limited/Kobalt Music Publishing Limited/Eternal Dance Media.
All Rights Reserved. International Copyright Secured.

Story Of My Life

Words & Music by John Ryan, Jamie Scott, Julian Bunetta, Harry Styles,
Niall Horan, Liam Payne, Louis Tomlinson & Zayn Malik

Somewhere Only We Know

Words & Music by Richard Hughes, Tim Rice-Oxley
& Tom Chaplin

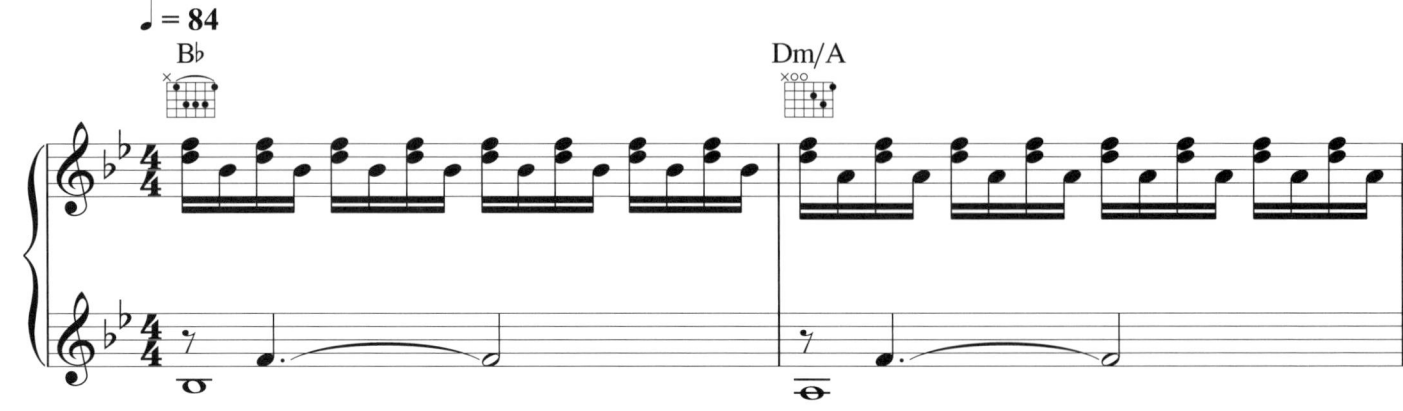

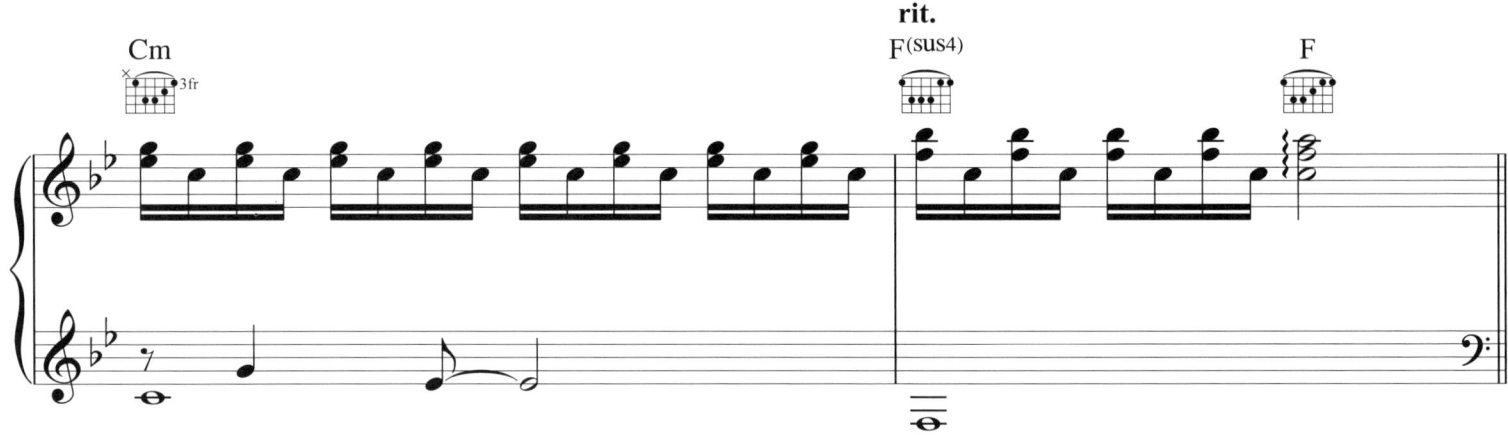

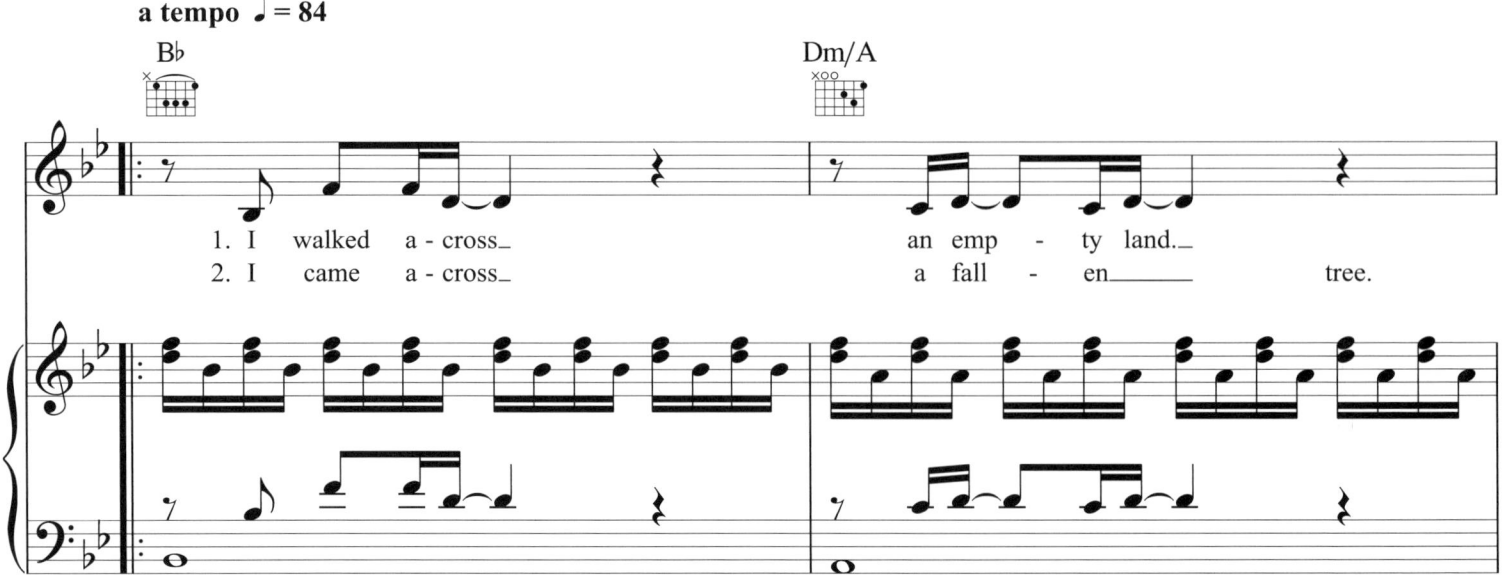

1. I walked across an empty land.
2. I came across a fallen tree.

© Copyright 2004 BMG Music Publishing Limited.
Universal Music Publishing MGB Limited.
All Rights Reserved. International Copyright Secured.

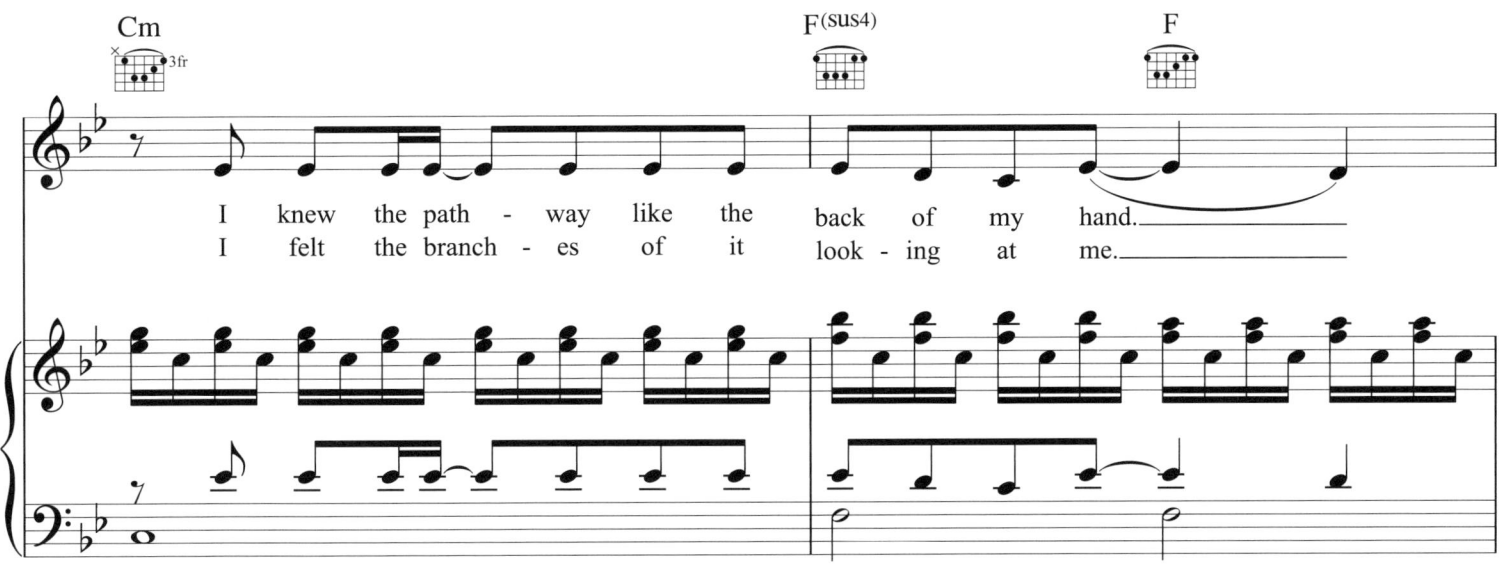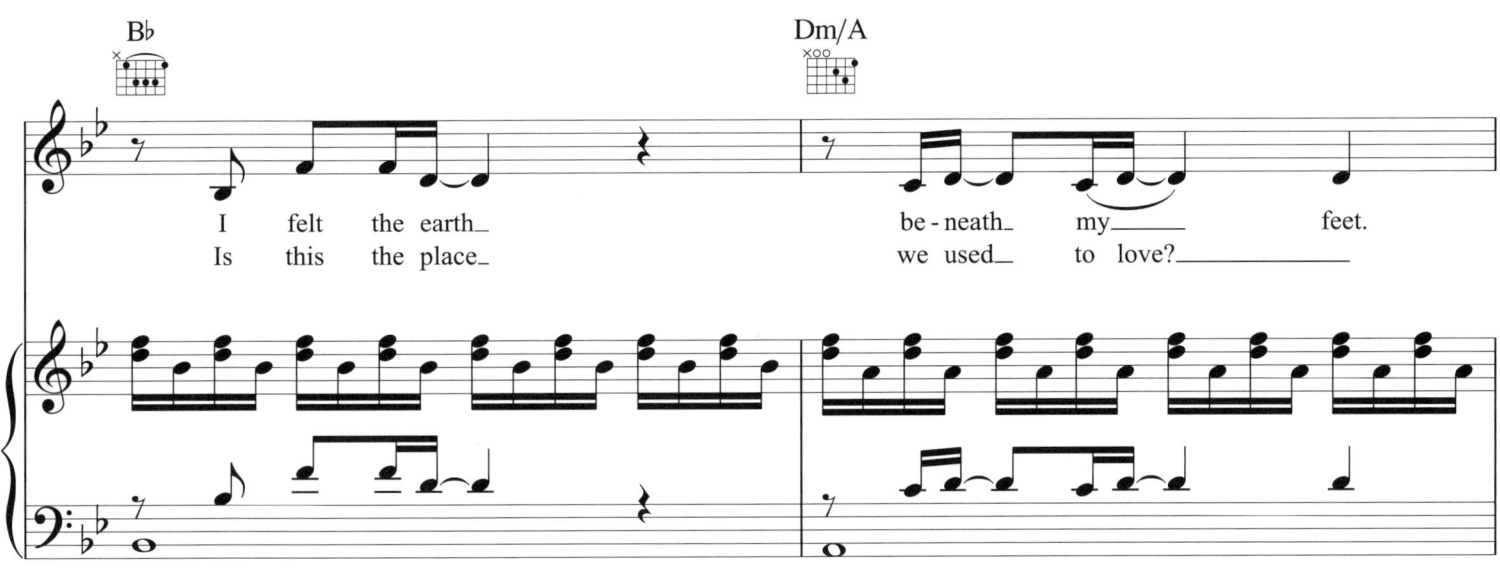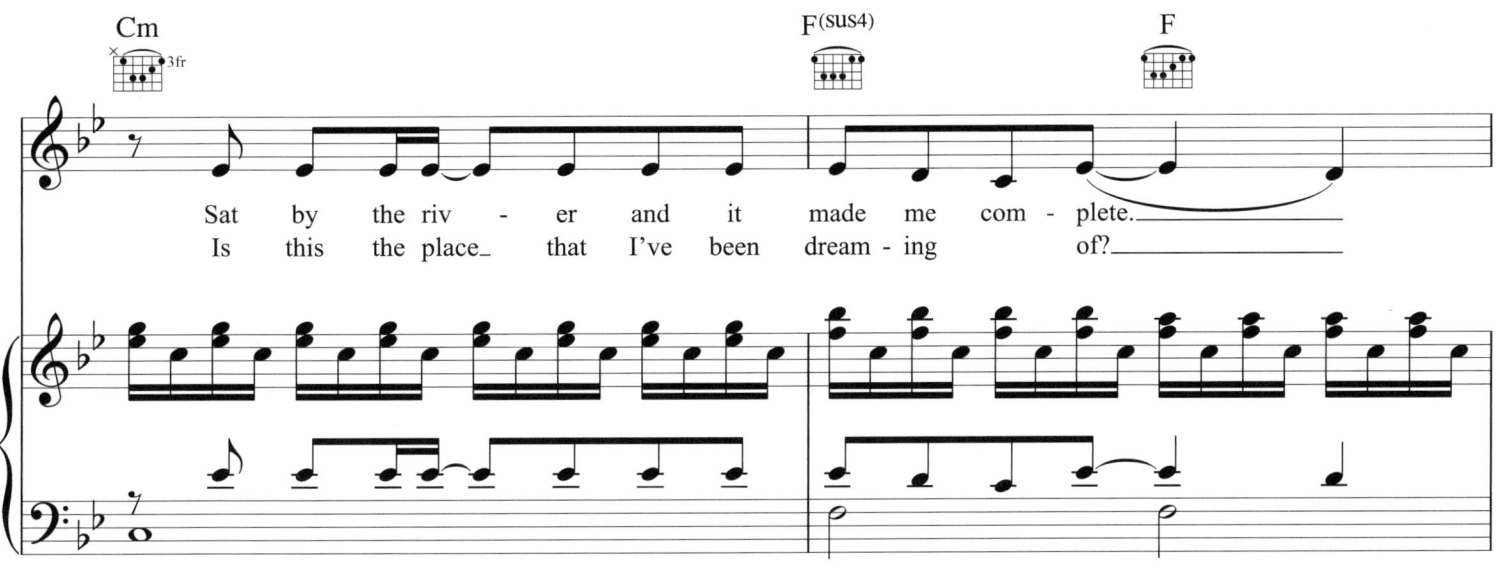

Trumpets

Words & Music by Jason Derulo & Jonathan Bellion

Unconditionally

Words & Music by Max Martin, Lukasz Gottwald,
Katy Perry & Henry Russell Walter

© Copyright 2013 Kasz Money Publishing/When I'm Rich You'll Be My Bitch/Prescription Songs/Oneirology Publishing/MXM Music AB.
Kobalt Music Publishing Limited/Warner/Chappell North America Limited.
All Rights Reserved. International Copyright Secured.

Bringing you the words and the music

All the latest music in print... rock & pop plus jazz, blues, country, classical and the best in West End show scores.

- Books to match your favourite CDs.

- Book-and-CD titles with high quality backing tracks for you to play along to. Now you can play guitar or piano with your favourite artist... or simply sing along!

- Audition songbooks with CD backing tracks for both male and female singers for all those with stars in their eyes.

- Can't read music? No problem, you can still play all the hits with our wide range of chord songbooks.

- Check out our range of instrumental tutorial titles, taking you from novice to expert in no time at all!

- Musical show scores include *The Phantom Of The Opera*, *Les Misérables*, *Mamma Mia* and many more hit productions.

- DVD master classes featuring the techniques of top artists.

Visit your local music shop or, in case of difficulty, contact the Marketing Department, Music Sales Limited, Newmarket Road, Bury St Edmunds, Suffolk, IP33 3YB, UK
marketing@musicsales.co.uk